LET'S MAKE A BETTER WORLD

DR SINGH'S INSIGHTS

LET'S MAKE A BETTER WORLD

DR SINGH'S INSIGHTS

DR BINAY SINGH

HTTPS://TWAGAA.COM

HTTPS://TWAGAA.COM

Mumbai, India
Website: https://twagaa.com
Email: hello@twagaa.com

First published by TWAGAA INTERNATIONAL

Title: Let's Make A Better World - Dr Singh's Insights
ISBN: 978-93-90488-18-6

First Edition
Published in India

Ordering Information:
Quantity sales: Special discounts are available on quantity purchases by corporations, associations, and others. For details, contact the publisher at the address or email above.

ACKNOWLEDGEMENTS

I have seen innumerable setbacks and triumphs in the world and have spent forty-four years facing challenges and refusing to give up. I write this book to inspire others to face life with the same spirit.

To my dear friend Billy, thank you very much for all your help.

To Yuliya, the better half of my friend Denis, thank you for writing the inspiring foreword to this book. It has been a blessing to know both of you for over 15 years.

FOREWORD

Do you often wonder where to start?

Your energy has no boundaries. Your desires and the possibilities that lay ahead of you too have no boundaries. We all are building our future today 'through our own choices'. Every small step we take is to move towards the life of our dreams.

This book 'Let's Make A Better World' by Dr Binay Singh will help you to launch your building block of positivity and live a wonderful life!

Yuliya Shapilova
Manager in a Tourist Company
Odessa, Ukraine

CONTENTS

UNDERSTANDING OUR SITUATION

In our world today, new problems seem to sneak up on us much faster than we can address them. As soon as we have gotten comfortable with the old problems, there are new ones ready to present themselves, ready to push us and to challenge us, demanding that we dig within ourselves to find the necessary strength to respond to them. This is the nature of a world that changes as rapidly as ours does; although we can count on progress, we can also count on setbacks. There is hardly any time to think about our situation – which makes it even more important for us to *make time* to do so.

After the last year, I believe few people would try to claim that our world today is free of problems. That is clearly not the case. Whether it is our economic lives or our personal lives, our political lives or our spiritual lives, there is plenty that we can do to make things better for ourselves. The problem is that it is not always clear to everyone what there is for us to do. As deeply as most people want to help and contribute positively, the details can become overwhelming. Those who approach our situation from the best of intentions are likely to burn themselves – if they do not work with the right set of tools.

The reality of our situation is that even though the problems seem external, they actually connect to the deepest parts of ourselves. Even something that seems surface-level, like unemployment, is a result of who we are as spiritual beings and how well we live and act from the heart. If we continue to think about these problems from a coldly rational perspective or assume that it is only a matter of reason, then we will run into the same pitfalls and wind up setting ourselves back more often than not.

To solve this, we need to encourage a total change in our worldview. Those of us who have seen each other from a sensible but inhuman point of view need to leave behind all of our old conceptions. Similarly, those of us who already see the world through warm and friendly eyes ought to find a way to inspire others to do the same. While these shifts may not be obvious when we first undertake them, they will pay off more than any specific plan we could chart out on a piece of paper or discuss in a meeting.

There are a few elements that define this shift most. These

elements, as I see them, define us as people. Without them we fail over and over, and with them we can't help but succeed – at everything that we do. The first element is love, the second element is empathy, and the third element is enthusiasm. Love, empathy, enthusiasm: look for these gifts inside yourself and then find a way to share them with others. *That* is how we correct our course and make today's world better and brighter. When we embrace each of these things, we can overhaul the entire system within which we live our lives.

This is about more than systems and policies, of course. We are talking about our one-to-one relationships, our visions for the future, and our hopes and dreams for the coming generations. If we let selfishness define us, then what *else* would we expect to define all these things? Without love, empathy, and enthusiasm, what would we predict for our world today other than *disaster*?

We have to treat people from these mindsets. When we find it difficult to express love and empathy to people or to follow through on our commitments enthusiastically, then the problem is with *us* – not with other people, not with our situation. This is how leaders see the world, viewing every moment as an opportunity to take responsibility, and if we cultivate leaders in love, empathy, and enthusiasm all around the world, then our situation will change from its very foundation.

We are not talking only about our best friends or our spouses or our children. This is a more exciting and more encompassing perspective of the world, one that considers each and every person. My wish is for all of us to see the world as our collective responsibility, for a person in America to think of the well-being of each person in India and for a person in Australia to think of the well-being of each person in Mexico. Just as our future becomes bigger, our world should become closer: the human community should someday feel like a single family.

Today, in the world, I see many people who would like to do as I do. These people would like to make the world a better place, to unite and gift the world their most stunning legacy. There is nothing holding them back, but because *some* people view these changes as impossible, others feel doubt and discouragement. To all the billion people who share my dream for our world today, let me say that *nothing* is impossible.

There is every reason for us to believe that we can inspire each other and motivate each other in this direction. We can look back on history and see that through the centuries, people have entered into higher levels of consciousness. Our natural state is one of progress, not regression, not stagnation. When we recognize that, then discouragement will make no sense to us. We will feel no doubt about all the wonders that are ahead of us in this world.

Through our courage, the fate of our world becomes clearer to us. We can ignore any uninspiring words and any lack of enthusiasm, thinking of them as short-lived phenomena, little in comparison to our strength and our potential. Then, we can get to work. We can put anything that would harm our emotional state or taint our visions behind us.

Remember that when we die, we can take none of our worldly possessions with us. In life, we should strive to leave it all out there, to let all our creativity and dreams pour outward and into the world. This is how we bestow our legacy on the world: in this book, as in all my other books, I am creating my legacy, which I know will live and go on even after I have breathed my last breath. This makes me happy, and if you find the same thing for yourself, it will make you happy as well.

It is my great pride and joy to see others smiling and successful, wanting for nothing and forever hopeful. That is what I want and how I feel: to need nothing, to doubt none of my dreams. If this sounds ambitious, all the better. The world today is the result of ambitious men and women who ignored all doubt and discouragement. Our forebears believed that what a mind can conceive, a mind can achieve. If you believe that too, then I am right there beside you, walking through today's world whistling a tune and tapping my feet along to the rhythm, hearing the music of life that lends its beauty to the future that is unfolding one moment at a time.

Now, I want to talk about what we need to do to make all this happen.

WHAT WE NEED TO DO

There is an important distinction for us to make when we talk about what we need to do to make today's world better than what it currently is. We are *not* talking about implementing a series of initiatives or coming up with an extensive plan. Instead, we are talking about something that cuts much deeper into how we view the world and what each of our actions means. We are reflecting on the nature of our actions – and what defines them in the first place. It may be more accurate, then, to say that we are talking about *why* we are doing what we need to do.

Toward that end, it is one of the great ironies of our time that most ambitious people tend to look outward too quickly, attempting to correct others and assuming that all the world's problems are a result of sins that their friends and neighbors are committing. While each of us shares in the responsibility for the situation of our world today, we can only think about ourselves. You can only think about yourself, and I can only think about myself. If we try to go any further too quickly, I assure you, we are going to miss something and do more harm than good.

What this means is that in order to change the world, you must first change yourself. Think about all of the failures and defects that you have noticed in others. This person rushes through tasks, and that person behaves unkindly. Both these observations may be true, but they are meaningless next to the more important truths that we can perceive about ourselves. If someone is unkind and someone else is thoughtless and I myself am lazy in the afternoons – where should my attention be?

The answer is *the latter*. Until I am a perfect person and as long as there is something about myself that I can correct, I need to start there.

Before you *can* change the world, you need to change yourself. To change others, you need to start from within. You need to develop the sort of mindset that always questions your own decisions and your own behaviors, thinking of ways that you could do better and of ways that you could be better so that you can then speak to people in a clearer and more inspiring tone. The people around you will see that you are "walking the talk" so to speak, that you are thinking of ways that you can improve yourself and not just casting judgments at everyone else in your life.

From there, you can change others. You can change the world. This may sound like a paradox to those who have never experienced it. *Why* should you be able to change the world if you direct all your energy and focus onto yourself? Why would that get you *anywhere*? It does, though. The more that you think about yourself and find ways that you can improve yourself, the more capably you will be able to address all the other problems in the world.

There is *no way* around this. If you try to change the world without changing yourself, you will find yourself shouting into a void. No one will listen to you, no one will hear you, and you will tire yourself out long before you have made a difference to anyone. You will waste all your time on a fruitless venture, thinking that because you see faults in others, you somehow deserve to correct those faults.

Let this sink in: you do *not* deserve to correct anyone else's faults unless you have first put in the work to correct your own faults. Until you have changed yourself, you can't change anything at all.

Hearing this, you may wonder what you need to do to look inward and shift yourself in the right directions. This is both simple and involved: to start changing yourself immediately, you can find a mentor who exhibits all the traits and behaviors that you want in yourself. If you see someone who is thriving in a career that you want for yourself, think about what they are doing and how you can adapt yourself to resemble them. Reflect on the skills that they have developed and try to come up with ways that you can develop the same skills in yourself.

There is more to this than the specific benefits, though. The humility that comes with receiving mentoring will enable you to see others from a more compassionate and empathetic point of view. You will see others' faults and then instead of lashing out at them, respond to them out of love. Remembering all the ways that you were insufficient before you found your mentor and before you started changing yourself, you will become more effective at changing others.

Once again, this may sound paradoxical to someone who has never gone through it before. It is not, though. The truth is that by making yourself quieter, subtler, softer, and humbler, you become stronger and more impactful. Your humility frees you to see the faults and shortcomings in others and then devise more creative ways to help them out of those faults and shortcomings.

I myself have chosen Sadhguru, Mahatma Gandhi, Nelson Mandela, and Mother Teresa as mentors. Each of these people has inspired me in some way, and by observing them, I have found shortcomings in myself. The work that goes into education is tiring and difficult at times, but from experience, I can tell you that it always pays off. What I have learned from my mentors is invaluable. They have imparted lessons to me, drawn from their lives, what I could have never learned through trial and error alone.

Once you have done sufficient work to change yourself, you can then look outward. You can think globally and put yourself into the bigger picture, reflecting on the changes that you have made in yourself and comparing them to changes that you would like to see in our entire situation. Say that you were once lacking in empathy: because you have corrected that, you can correct it in the entire world. You can perceive the lack of empathy in the whole population and slash through it, cutting it up into more manageable pieces so that it becomes less intimidating and less overwhelming for you.

This connects to who we are as people – both sides of it, the rush to change *everything* and our aversion to changing ourselves. When we grapple with both these sides of ourselves, we can think more selflessly and sincerely. We can start to think about the world in simpler and more lucid terms, generating solutions from a more grounded mindset. Thinking in concrete terms, we can avoid losing ourselves in dreams of success and jealousy toward others for *their* success.

In short, we can see things as they are and then feel happiness in our hearts. Rather than fake happiness, putting on a smile and hoping that no one can tell the difference between it and the real thing, we can let endless joy and energy flow through us.

This makes intuitive sense to us, but make no mistake: it is *rare*.

Take Elvis, for example. He was a historic success, reaching the heights of the music industry and setting a standard that none of his predecessors would match. People showed up for his concerts by the thousands, and in every soda shop and every living room, his records were played. He was still unhappy, though, because he never learned how to think of himself before he thought of the world. Ignoring himself, he missed that lesson, failing to pick up on the skills that he needed to handle his position.

Start small, accept your own limitations, believe that you *can* change, and then do it. Then and only then will you be able to aim higher and think about the changes that you would like to see in our world today.

Next, let's dive deeper into the methods and strategies that we can use to do what we need to do.

HOW WE NEED TO ACT

There is a certain urgency around our situation in the world today. We cannot deny this any more than we can deny that there are problems all around us. When we think about what is at stake – our loved ones, our neighbors, *all* of our happiness – we should feel motivation coursing through our bodies. It should push us to see the world in brighter colors and to understand that there is no time to hesitate. There is certainly no room for us to make any mistakes either. We need to get moving and stay moving, never stopping until our lives have come to an end and we can say honestly to the next generation, "We have given our all to this, and we are proud of the work that we have done."

Urgency, in this case, is a positive thing. It becomes a negative, though, when we let it get ahead of us. If urgency starts to hold us back or trip us up, then it no longer serves its purpose. The emotion that should be moving us forward is, in that case, preventing us from reaching our full potential. Instead of urgency reminding us of the importance of our vision, it keeps us from our vision altogether. Before we have made the changes that we need to make in our world today, we stumble over ourselves, looking for big changes that will never come, frustrated and distraught whenever the little changes show themselves.

To overcome this, we need to accept the power of gradual change. We need to find the balance between urgency and calm, accepting that the importance of our vision will send our hearts racing *without* allowing that to fluster us. This is a difficult task, one with which people have struggled for centuries. If you can succeed in this area, then you can leverage all the energy and power of your most urgent moments into real results, turning the momentum that would have become an annoyance into a boost forward, thrusting you toward the mindset changes that are going to mean the most to you in the long term.

If I say I want to change the world *today*, it's too much. If I say I want to change the world in thirty years, on the other hand, that is doable. Thirty years may seem like a long time, but if a group of people is thinking this way, then even gradual change becomes tremendous. Think about it: change one person a day for thirty years, and you wield the impact of more than 100,000 people. If each of those 100,000 people can do the same, then we are talking about a global scale. At that point, *everyone* in the world will be working toward change, viewing the world as a flexible thing and viewing our collective selves as an accessible tool.

That is worldwide change: it starts with one person, and out of one person, it expands rapidly.

None of this is theoretical. We can observe this reality every single day. We are all living in energy, and to create the world around us, we have to move that energy. When we move it positively, encouraging each other and fostering positivity, then our communities become stronger. Living in positive energy, we can generate inspiration without limits. We can create inspiration, turning it into a commodity instead of waiting around for someone else to create it. Those people can do the same, creating energy, turning it into commodities of their own.

The positivity becomes *undeniable.*

To see this in action, look at Norway. There, the government offers people high-quality facilities and desirable opportunities. There is no reason for corruption and no reason for bribes because the people know that everything they want is within their reach. Norwegians would never think of cheating each other because they recognize that they are working together as one *and* that they are individuals, each of whom is capable of changing himself or herself. They are working from the inside-out, thriving because their worldview is in sync with reality.

When you think this way, positive energy becomes unavoidable. Groups begin to work cohesively because no one expects anything or makes any unreasonable demands from anyone else. We are operating in the way that makes the most sense – and thus, trying to *change the world* in the way that makes the most sense.

There is an old saying that is relevant here: God helps those who help themselves. If there are billions of people worldwide helping themselves while also living from a place of love, empathy, and enthusiasm, then our situation *will* change overnight. The very idea that was once absurd, to change *everything all at once*, becomes attainable in this way.

There is no caveat to this, nothing that we need to profess and no philosophy that we need to adopt. We can all believe different things and do different things. That is okay, as long as we think globally and in unity. If we view the world positively, the energy will move regardless of anything else. No matter what we say our religion is or how we describe our nationalities, today's world becomes a better place thanks to this simple shift.

I say "simple" in the sense that this shift is straightforward. It is, of course, not easy. In today's world, there are wars, there is poverty, and there is suffering. These are giant problems. Even worse, they are likely to continue on for several decades at least. The old truth holds, though: it is better to have a bad peace than a good war. Even though it will take work and sacrifice, it is preferable for us to overcome our old faults than to accept them as the "norm."

In chaos, there is hope for all of this. The pandemic has

compelled all of us to think about the environment and how we can find balance in our world. Coronavirus has pushed people toward empathy, encouraging us to think about others on the other side of the planet, those whom we would have never thought about before.

While we should hope that it doesn't take a pandemic for us to rethink all of our outdated ideas, we *do* have to rethink our system and our society. If we can do this and make sense of urgency and patience *together*, we can address our problems.

It starts with you – and your willingness to learn and grow. As I have said, "Everyone needs mentors while making business or life decisions to be inspired to reach greatness. They are the best to tell you where you need to improve and where you cannot. The true mentor uplifts and enriches. So ensure you choose your mentors very carefully. There's nothing more helpful than a mentor who inspires and simplifies your life."

TODAY'S NEW WORLD

All of this talk about the problems in our world today may lead you to believe that I am pessimistic about our situation. I am anything *but* pessimistic, though. Throughout this year, I have launched new ventures and expanded old ones, building on my ideas for the future and striving toward my most ambitious dreams.

On my 44th birthday, I published my 44th book. This was a milestone for me. I shared it with my friends, family, and colleagues, and all throughout my birthday week, I received words of congratulations and encouragement. The people closest to me reminded me how much there is for us to feel optimistic about in the world. In spite of all of our problems, they have reminded me that there is far more that is exciting and positive than there is discouraging and negative.

While today's world is full of problems, it is full of *problem solvers* too.

The work that I am putting into my vision for the world is only one piece of all this. I know entrepreneurs, activists, artists, and other leaders, all of whom would never stop to think that our collective situation would prevent them from living out their dreams. They have done and they are doing the work to change themselves, overcoming one problem after another, embracing their own power and potential. They inspire me and others to do the same.

If you too feel passionate about your vision for the world, you are already changing today's world. As long as your desires and your beliefs encourage you, then no war, no pandemic, and no recession can hold you back. Our world today, for all of its shortcomings, is the perfect stage for you to play out your greatest performance and live your greatest life – and I for one am *ecstatic* to witness it all.

I share your enthusiasm for our world. Every day, new experiences energize me. I am optimistic that these experiences are lessons, never annoyances, never distractions. If people see you and me and think that we are living our lives on another level, that is *fine*. We can make our lives as beautiful as we want them to be and then wait for the rest of the world to catch up with us.

When they do catch up with us, they will see that we have been living in the future all along. We have been living out the meaning of life in all our actions, hoping that they would catch on and wishing that they would join us.

On the day that they do join us, they will become leaders just as we are. They will, as leaders do, think about others before they think of themselves but judge themselves before they judge others. Offering positivity to the world, they will understand that life is spectacular regardless of all our problems and that our world is impressive in spite of any faults that we find in it.

This continues onward endlessly. I see that after this pandemic, the world will go on. Life will go on. In my book *Coronavirus: Opportunity through Adversity*, I talked about this idea in detail. The way I see it, the pandemic is gifting us with lessons about balance. There is no reason to fight this or to feel discouraged by it because we are *learning* from it. Every day of this pandemic, we are growing as people and blossoming as the incredible human community that we can be.

This does not mean that we can go on and live our lives the way that we have been living them. The planet is crying out to us, after all. Any time we destroy nature, we destroy our own lives. We should understand that God created us to love each other and to live life. It is a gift, but it is a responsibility too. We can live our lives feeling free and happy – only if we are willing to accept that we owe a debt to each other and to the world around us as well.

To understand all this, to make sense of today's world, think about the children of the next generation and what they are going to think of us. Would you like them to hear *bad* stories about yourself?

Of course not!

We want the next generation to look back on us gratefully, knowing that we were cognizant of them and that everything we did, we did because we wanted to leave them something worthwhile. When they read about our challenges in history books, we want them to read about the solutions right alongside them, learning from us the way that we have from each other.

In 2020, all this came home to me. I faced many different obstacles – and found a way around them all. This has boosted my energy and positivity. I am willing to die for the world, to sacrifice for it, to keep sacrificing for it. I will always give myself completely to this world, thinking about my lifestyle, my actions, and my priorities. I will try to find a way forward when I feel stuck, and I will not let my energy stop from moving me onward.

Think about *your* lifestyle, *your* actions, *your* priorities. Make the world a place of love, empathy, and enthusiasm. Start with yourself and then let the energy flow out to all the people around you. This is what I aim to do: I would like to inspire China, India, US, all countries, to associate with each other, to unite and make the world better for us all, for our children, for our future.

That will be the *new* world.

I am sincerely working for people, 100%. I know that because I am living out positivity, it will come back to me. The energy that I have gifted to the world will find its way back into my heart and back into my hands so that I can cultivate it further and turn it into something more.

In today's world, the moment is as it always is, an ever-moving thing, and to keep up with it, we need to acknowledge that we are ever-moving too. Live your life in such a way that you respect this ideal. Keep learning *every day* and find the humility that you need to become a source of inspiration to others.

Today's world is *not* a static thing. The problems that affect us today will start to dissipate and even disappear. They will become things of the past, remnants of an era gone by, reminders of what we once were and of how far we have come. Thinking back a year, five years, or ten years, you may see this process in your own life.

Embrace it, cherish it, love it, and *live* it. It is reality, it is *undeniable.*

ABOUT THE AUTHOR

Dr Binay Kumar Singh, Founder & CEO of *Singh Marine Management Ltd.* in Odessa, Ukraine, and Founder & President of *Federation of Global Maritime Community*, is an entrepreneur, author, and public speaker. His life mission is to serve the world's communities and guide everyone through positivity, love, and enthusiasm. This is reflected in his simple and timeless life philosophy: "Treat people as you like to be treated."

Dr Singh has a Master of Science in Marine Navigation and a Doctorate of Philosophy. He is a globally recognized expert in international shipping with over two decades of experience. Dr Singh is also taking wonderful measures for the needy community of the society as well. His new project with the name "Selfless fund" is specifically targeted to help those who are in need. Dr Singh has also launched his new company GSR which is going to bring innovations to the shipping and maritime industry. His efforts for the shipping industry as well as for the society is an example of his generosity and selflessness.

He enjoys pursuing multiple passions like singing, dancing, playing the piano and the accordion, and keeping healthy by practicing yoga and CrossFit.

https://drbinaysingh.com

MORE BOOKS BY DR BINAY SINGH

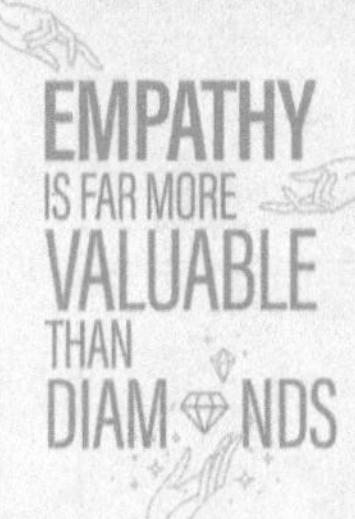

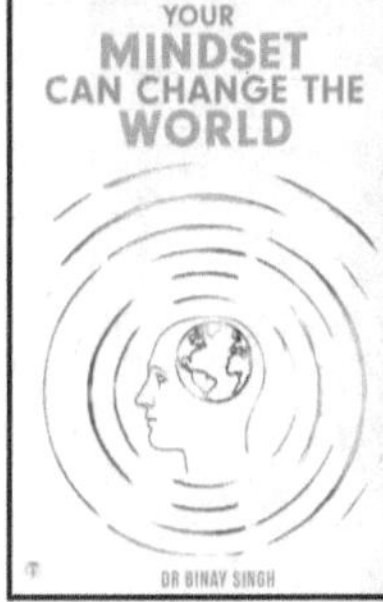

THE ART OF
MARITIME MANNING
MY INSIGHTS
DR BINAY SINGH

THE
ART
OF
NEGOTIATION
DR SINGH'S INSIGHTS
DR BINAY SINGH

THE
ART
OF
SMARTPHONE-LIFE BALANCE
DR SINGH'S INSIGHTS
DR BINAY SINGH

ODESSA
MY CITY, MY HOME
DR BINAY SINGH

DIGITAL ADDICTION
KEEP YOURSELF AND YOUR FAMILY SAFE
DR BINAY SINGH

THE
ART
OF
TEAM MANAGEMENT
DR SINGH'S INSIGHTS
DR BINAY SINGH

THE
ART
OF
LEADERSHIP AT SEA
DR SINGH'S INSIGHTS
DR BINAY SINGH

SHIPS &
RELATIONSHIPS
DR BINAY SINGH

MY
FANTASTIC
VOYAGE
TO
ODESSA
DR BINAY SINGH

THE ART OF
GIVING
DR SINGH'S INSIGHTS
GIVE
DR BINAY SINGH

A MESSAGE TO
YOUNG SEAFARERS
DR SINGH'S INSIGHTS
DR BINAY SINGH

Svetlana
my love forever
DR BINAY SINGH

THE
ART
OF
MOTIVATIONAL
SPEAKING
DR SINGH'S INSIGHTS
DR BINAY SINGH

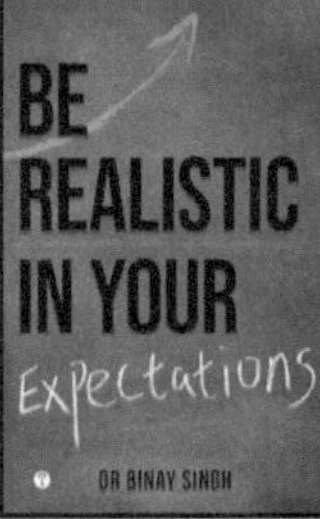
BE
REALISTIC
IN YOUR
Expectations
DR BINAY SINGH

The
TRUE MEANING OF
HOPE
DR BINAY SINGH

AVOIDING
DISTRACTIONS
ACHIEVING
SUCCESS
DR SINGH'S INSIGHTS
DR BINAY SINGH

THE
ART
OF
TIME MANAGEMENT
DR SINGH'S INSIGHTS
DR BINAY SINGH

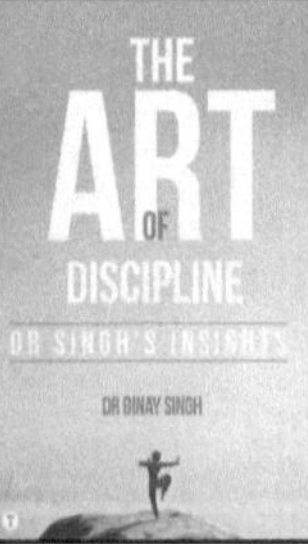
THE
ART
OF
DISCIPLINE
DR SINGH'S INSIGHTS
DR BINAY SINGH

Care
WITH YOUR
WORDS
DR BINAY SINGH

MR POSITIVE
DR SINGH'S GUIDE TO
LIVING YOUR BEST LIFE

THE
Magic
OF MUSIC
DR SINGH'S INSIGHTS
DR BINAY SINGH

DR SINGH'S GUIDE TO
REAL HAPPINESS
DR BINAY SINGH

THE NEW
MARITIME WAY
DR BINAY SINGH

DR SINGH'S GUIDE TO
REAL SUCCESS
DR BINAY SINGH

THE NEW ERA OF
BUSINESS
TRAINING
DR BINAY SINGH

www.ingramcontent.com/pod-product-compliance
Lightning Source LLC
LaVergne TN
LVHW101933220826
846093LV00009B/444

* 9 7 8 9 3 9 0 4 8 8 1 8 6 *